RECONNET WITH LIFE

RECONNECT WITH LIFE

Sangeeta Kabra

YASH PUBLICATIONS
Delhi-110032

RECONNECT WITH LIFE

Sangeeta Kabra

ISBN : 978-93-85647-95-6

First Edition : 2023

Published by : Yash Publications
1/10753, Street No. 3, Subhash Park,
Naveen Shahdara, Delhi-110032 (India)

Contact : +91 9599483887
E-mail: yashpublicationdelhi@gmail. com
Website: www. yashpublications.co.in
Avilable at : *amazon. in, flipkart. com*

Typeset by : G. R. Sharma, Delhi

PREFACE

Dear reader,

This book is an account of my personal experiences and insights in my own mind. For years, I have been exploring deep bottoms in my mind, searching for the ways to have more love, happiness and better relationships in my life. This is the ultimate result of my searching for years.

As I believe, man has the potential to make his life either heaven or hell. The destiny of a man is in his own hands, not elsewhere. The destiny is what a man crafts for himself. Nothing more. He has the potential to make his destiny whatever he needs.

As I have seen for years, all of us are able to change our entire life and make it better with simple positive changes in every day life.

Finally, all of us are here, in this world, to gain more love, happiness and better relationships in our life, aren't we? Right here, with these simple lessons, you will indeed have more love, happiness and better relationships in your life.

You will follow one simple way a day and have amazing results. You will certainly transform yourself to the next level. You will feel more successful and accomplished. Simply, you will transform your life with this ultimate guide.

After reading this, you will change the way you think, the way you see the world and the way you understand happenings to you. You will lead a happy life.

With unconditional love

Sangeeta Kabra

Acknowledgement

How do you feel about your life today?

Do you live every day in excitement?

Do you look forward to what's coming up next?

Are you living your best life?

If your answer to any of the above is a no, not sure, or maybe, that means you're not living your life to the fullest. Which really shouldn't be the case, because your life experience is yours to create.

We all have good days and bad days, and the most important thing is to make the best out of each day, regardless of the good or bad. Ultimately, we only have one life to live. We can't control all the bad things that happen, but we can change our attitude towards them and in the process, shape our future and create our most amazing life experience.

A philosophy of life is an overall vision or attitude toward life and the purpose of it. Human activities are limited by time, and death.

But we forget this.

We fill up our time with distractions, never asking whether they are important, whether we really find them of value.

Without a personal philosophy, we end up living without direction.

To connect to life is to connect to every aspect of our lives. Most important of all is to connect to ourselves, and to our own movement within life. That is, to connect to our body and our mind, to connect to spirituality, to our stage in life, to connect to the natural rhythms that guide us, and to connect to death and dying – a natural part of life.

So many of us do not connect to life. We search for something not knowing what it is. We search for happiness and fulfilment. But we search in the outer world not realising that we find these things by looking within.

The most difficult part of connecting to life is to slow our mind enough to even see what we need to do.

By finding ways to feel more connected to life, you'll boost confidence and happiness for greater health and satisfaction, long-term.

At times I can get stressed too. Yet, by taking the time to reflect on what's important and how best I can remove myself from the stress, and do something that will boost my mood and energy, I start feeling more love and peace all around.

Whether it's through healthy habits, like exercise or reading, or by meeting up with friends after work to catch up, doing something to increase happiness when you're feeling vulnerable should do the trick.

Why is connecting with life important?

If you want to spend your life in a way that makes sense for you, if you want to live your own journey, then you need to be connected to yourself. By putting self-connection first, you will make the choices that keep you on your path, you'll enjoy more confidence, feel more at peace, receive more insights, have better relationships, and, perhaps best of all, you'll believe in and trust yourself.

How do you know if you are disconnected from life?

Some common signs that you are disconnected and that your relationship with yourself needs attention are chronic self-doubt, low self-confidence, a harsh inner-voice, negative self-image, a pattern of dysfunctional relationships, lack of purpose in life, constant anxiety, unhealthy lifestyle, and emotional instability.

In a world where we are encouraged to focus on the life we create 'out there' and to in turn neglect the world 'in here', many of us are left cut off from our inner worlds and from our deepest selves.

The consequence is a continual sense of dissatisfaction and frustration, because even when we achieve and acquire what we desired, we are still left feeling empty and unfulfilled.

This challenges our sense of worthiness, as our self-worth is mistakenly hinged upon external achievement, validation, and recognition. But your self-worth isn't contingent upon doing or having anything but a connection to life and ourselves.

To be connected to life allows you to go out into the world with the embodied awareness of your inherent self-worth. No energy is spent seeking external sources of inner worthiness. No energy is used up trying to earn your own love.

The truth is, how far in the right direction you go in the outer world is in direct proportion to how deeply connected you are in the inner world. Are you ready to go deep and discover what's possible?

Here are 31 ways to feel more loved and connected to your world, where you can get back to *really* living it.

CONTENT

Preface 5

Acknowledgement 7

1. Listen to your heart 13
2. Love unconditionally 16
3. Live Each Day to the Fullest 19
4. Find Moments of Relaxation 22
5. Stay Positive 25
6. Be open to humor- Smile more 28
7. Follow a healthy lifestyle 31
8. Surround yourself with positive people 35
9. Gratitude Rocks 38
10. Practice Forgiveness 41
11. Stop and smell the roses 44
12. Celebrate Life 47
13. Just Do It! 50

14. Balance the elements of life 53
15. Enjoy the Journey 56
16. Create Space 58
17. Support Yourself With Loving Thoughts 61
18. Explore Your Spirituality 64
19. Get into Nature 69
20. Make time for what you love 71
21. Get Back to Your Basics 74
22. Really listen to others 77
23. No regret 79
24. Tap your creative self 81
25. Never Stop, Keep Improving 84
26. Be Emotionally Intelligent 88
27. Get rid of things that are weighing you down 90
28. Deepen Your Connections with Others 93
29. Scroll less, live more 96
30. Try New Things 98
31. Nurture your inner child 101
32. Let go of comparison 103
33. Set healthy boundaries with others 106
34. Appreciate yourself more 109
35. Value yourself by valuing your time 111
36. Discover your core values 114
37. Create Perfect Solitude 118
38. Cultivate Self Discipline 121
39. Spread Kindness & Develop Empathy 124
40. Give Back, for No Reason at All 127

Summary 131

LISTEN TO YOUR HEART

"Have the courage to follow your heart and intuition. They somehow already know what you truly want to become. The rest is secondary."

— SPJ

A few years back, on a beautiful evening, I was sitting on a bench in the park, relaxing watching the stars. . For years, I have been searching for the ways to live better and achieve more in life. Suddenly there was a flash in my mind, which was the guiding light for me.

My heart said no more waiting, now you should do something to make your life and your loved ones meaning full. And I started writing, I started posting on social media by writing small articles that can help us to make our life meaningful. After this, I started getting affection and praise from the people.

And then I started writing this book, I ever wanted to write about life and I listened to my heart since it better knew what was best for me, always. So from that day, I started writing this book.

After few years, I received an another call from my heart, to work for society by empowering people to manage their own lives, promoting people's independence, supporting people's social inclusion and participation in society and helping people to keep safe and well and I started working as a social worker and started an organisation for people in need. And happiness, I'm attaining on regular and daily basis is eternal.

Have you ever had such a sudden thought in your mind? When your heart has told you, what is the purpose of your life? And what will bring you true happiness?

Did you hear that voice and act on it.

If not, don't mind if you missed one chance to happiness. It will give you a second call.

I believe that all of us have many chances to make our life meaningful. Our life and universe itself keeps sending us those signals to act upon them.

Colors, flowers, numbers, animals, feathers, rocks, and crystals all have certain meanings.

Pay attention to what you see, what you come into contact with, what keeps reappearing in your life, and what you're drawn to. When you feel like "this is right" or "something is off" or "every part of me wants to do this," that's a clear sign from the universe.

Living a heart-based life is not going to eliminate all of your problems, but it will give you a flashlight when the lights go out.

So, never ignore any signal coming in your way. It can be your gold mine. Your way to wealth.

And to be honest, I don't see any other way to live life if you want to tap into deep contentment and joy.

Here are the biggest benefits I've noticed in my life

The most obvious benefit is happiness.

I worry less. I have more time to stop and smell the flower moments. I trust life and my heart.

I no longer try to figure everything out. I don't try to control my life as much. It's a huge stress reliever.

At the same time, I use both my mind and my heart to navigate through life and to tap into more happiness, joy, and fulfillment.

I used to be in constant battle with life. When something went wrong, I tried to fix it.

I've come to trust that I don't have to hurry to accomplish things in order to be happy. I can be happy now if I take a breath and relax.

Following your heart doesn't mean your life becomes a fairy tale. But when I listen to my heart, I realize that whatever happens is okay.

The more I follow my heart, the more fulfilled I feel.

The difference is that I've grown to trust life and to trust my heart. But I'm still human. And I'm still learning.

Remember, this is not a race.

It all starts right here by listening to your heart and living life one moment at a time.

LOVE UNCONDITIONALLY

"Unconditional love really exists in each of us. It is part of our deep inner being. It is not so much an active emotion as a state of being."

— *Ram Dass*

Here I am talking to you about one of the most incredible feelings that you could ever experience – unconditional love. The unconditional love, the truest of all forms.

The term unconditional love does not mean love without limits or bounds. It means, "I offer you my love freely without condition." This means that when we offer our love, we offer it without expectation of repayment. It is important to offer this type of unconditional love.

Love is not just a warm fuzzy feeling. It is a deep and strong affection we feel for another person, expressed through words and actions.

We seek love from friends, family members and a romantic partner, but sometimes we tend to place too many conditions on these relationships, causing us to miss out on the power of love.

For example, we may feel that we are only able to love those who love us in return or only until they are no longer meeting our expectations. But true love is unconditional.

When we truly care for another individual, we must continue to do so in the good times and the bad. All relationships face obstacles and limitations, but if we overcome them, we experience the amazing gift of love.

Every time we hear a love story turned cold, mostly the culprit has been expectation.

More we walk along the journey of love, more we start expecting from other person. And when those expectations aren't met, we lose interest in love, we lose the capacity to love.

It happened with me too, lots of expectations, questions and bitter experiences of breaking ups.

If you're not perfect, you can't expect others to be.

When the time passed and I became mature, now, I can say, Unconditional love, is love without strings attached. It's love you offer freely.

Unconditional love binds people, strengthens relationships, keeps people connected, makes us powerful and heal the world.

What if we didn't keep any expectations in the first place?

What if we never cared about what we are getting back, or how they react, and just love them?

Just love them, because we love to love them. Nothing they do affect our love for them in our hearts.

This kind of love is the fresh air, huge relief. There is no winning or losing in this love. Only love is there, that is all consuming and life transforming.

The answer is to love without expectation, and show compassion for and acceptance of others.

Unselfish love is expressed for everyone around us, animals included. A show of kindness, mercy, care or a word of concern are ways in which we can express love.

Spread unconditional love to your family, friends, spouse, parents, children, pets and humanity. You don't need to be a great personality for that. You just have to share your time, love and true feelings among people to make them happy.

In this way, love becomes more free-flowing and fun and more fulfilling.

Live Each Day to the Fullest

Every day, it's important to ask and answer these questions: "What's good in my life?" and "What needs to be done?"

— Nathaniel Branden

As the saying goes, "Live life to the fullest!"

Live today – Always live each day as if it were your last. Enjoy every moment of your life and have everything you wish.

Recently a friend of mine had a heart attack. She is a very successful business woman and a well-known personality of the society.

After this incident, she realised that she could not give time to her family in for material gains. Many of us live life like that and regret one day not to live fully.

I don't want to die as a a well known author or one of the richest women lived in this world.

I will rather die as a person, who lived life fully and understood its secrets. Material objectives are important. But, living your life fully comes first. We are here for it.

Whether it's taking care of your children, working hard on your career, writing a new blog post each day, or baking up fabulous creations, you get to decide how you enjoy spending your time.

Your parents, friends, community, and society in general all have their opinions, but at the end of the day, you're the only person who will be around for every moment of your life.

Start thinking about how to make your day perfect. Spend quality time with your loved ones, walk in nature and do what you like the most.

You may be thinking then why is it that people stop themselves from living fully. People put up a wall thinking they can't do anything. Most of the time it is dwelling on the past.

Let the past not mingle with the present. Don't live a life full of regrets. Life is too short so you must make the most out of it.

Do what makes you happy, and everything else will fall into place. This may not mean finding your perfect job if you're limited by education, location, or job openings. However, you can still do what you love by engaging in hobbies, volunteer work, or mentoring.

There are many ways to create a happy full life. You can replacing a bad though by a good one,

Make a list of things you want to do before you die,

Live day by day.

Go to new places.

Reflect on the things you have to accomplished.

Accept people for who they are.

Be realistic with the goals you set, and the most cliché of them all Listen to your heart, you will always find the best choice.

Learning to live life to the fullest is a big step in discovering a path that will lead you to your greatest sense of happiness and accomplishment.

We all need moments to rest and relish in a sense of contentment, but staying in one place too long will leave you feeling a lack in life. Discover what makes your life feel meaningful and go after it.

Remember, Nobody can go back and start a new beginning, but anyone can start today and make a new ending. Make an effort to enjoy every moment; take every day as a new life experience and live it fully.

FIND MOMENTS OF RELAXATION

"Calm mind brings inner strength and self-confidence, so that's very important for good health."

—Dalai Lama.

We are in the age of technology. Our today's life, which is full of many amenities. Still, We have become a part of the blind race of materialism, which has hurt our mental peace and contentment.

is this happening to you too?

If yes,

I believe that this is a question of everyone's concern including me.

Let's figure out how we can overcome this stress.

One of my clients shared her experience with me, that she feels very stressed because of her past negative experiences and expectations for personal and professional achievements.

Most of times, she feels that her life is worthless because of not being able to fulfill those expectations. Then I also recalled my past when I also felt the same challenge in my professional life.

I found myself anxious about going to work every day, thoughts crowding my brain as soon as my head hit the pillow to sleep, amplifying immediately after waking up.

Then, I have been introduced to the part of myself that is underneath my conscious mind. it's a place of peace and serenity. And I honestly find it hard to believe how I haven't indulged in it before now.

And this is what happened when I started practicing relaxation techniques like meditation, mindfulness, yoga, singing, dancing and talking to my loved ones. I started meditating every day after my work hours, even during busy weekends.

When faced with many responsibilities and tasks or the demands of an illness, relaxation techniques may not be a priority in your life. But that means you might miss out on the health benefits of relaxation.

According to Psychology Today, meditation is the strongest mental practice that has the power to reset our happiness set points.

I personally experienced this shift by doing meditation only for 20 mins a day, when I felt unfulfilled by the external world around me and started looking for happiness within. Every day I began doing meditations for joy and happiness, began to stop and pause during the day to go inward, and just be present with my inner self. It was nothing short of magical.

The tasks challenged my beliefs and ideas, the meditation sessions explored different ideas on abundance, gratitude, spiritualism and letting go.

Overtime, I felt as if a weight had been lifted off me; my social anxiety was dropping and I began living life for me and no one else. In fact, this time of my life was so meaningful that it inspired me to become a life coach and an author.

I believe meditation and any other relaxation technique may be the key to unlocking happiness, is the deep connection we may get with our inner self. In my experience, those who meditate report feeling more content with who they are, what they have and feel they have more clarity in life.

It is also during a deep meditation practice that you can connect deeply with atman, or the true self, which according to yoga philosophy, is where pure happiness resides and how we create a direct line of communicating with our soul and intuition.

So maybe the next time you're feeling like you need a happiness boost instead of looking outward, try gazing inward and give meditation a chance and stay stress free.d contentment.

STAY POSITIVE

"Train your mind to see the good in every situation."

—Unknown

In our life, we have all received well-intentioned advice to stay positive. Sometimes it can be hard to stay positive in life when you are drowning in the waters of negativity.

Happiness isn't the only type of **positivity definition**. There are many ways to stay positive in your life, even when you're experiencing anger, sadness, or challenges. The definition of being positive is having hope and confidence in one's ability to handle what's tough, along with remembering that nothing is all negative all the time.

Over the years, as a Holistic Life coach, I've also done a lot of research on the positive effects of being positive and the negative effects of being negative.

The research is clear. It really does pay to be positive and the benefits include enhanced health and longevity, happiness, career advancement, athletic performance, team building and financial success. Being positive is not just a nice way to live. It's the way to live.

Being positive is not just a nice way to live. It's the way to live. And to explain this fact, I am sharing a very familiar story with you.

Some hundred years back, a man was reading a morning newspaper when he saw his name in the obituary column. In the newspaper, there was the wrong person's name in the death section. He was shocked to read his name in that column.

So he tried to find out what was written about his death. The obituary read, "Dynamite King Dies." And also, "He was the merchant of death." This man was the inventor of dynamite, and when he read the words "merchant of death,." The man asked himself, "Is this how I am going to be remembered?"

He thought hard and decided that this was not how he wanted to be remembered. So from that day on, he started working toward peace. His name was Alfred Nobel. He is remembered today for the great Nobel Prize.

Like Alfred Nobel worked upon his emotions and gave new meaning to his values, we also can do the same.

The moral of this attitude story is to introspect yourself and work upon your beliefs. It will help bring more happiness and positivity into your life.

This story also inspired me to always keep my perspective positive and change myself accordingly, no matter what gift life gives us.

View everyone and everything as being supportive of you. This simple shift of viewpoint can create miracles.

Positive thinking doesn't mean that you ignore life's less

pleasant situations. Positive thinking just means that you approach unpleasantness in a more positive and productive way. You think the best is going to happen, not the worst.

Having a positive outlook enables you to cope better with stressful situations, which reduces the harmful health effects of stress on your body.

With practice and with my experience I can assure you, when your state of mind is generally optimistic, you're better able to handle everyday stress in a more constructive way. That ability may contribute to the widely observed health benefits of positive thinking.

Be open to humor-Smile more

"Like a welcome summer rain, humor may suddenly cleanse and cool the earth, the air and you."

–Langston Hughes

A client came to me for his first counseling session. He had a bag full of vegetables in both of his hands, but looked so gloomy and tired.

Help! the client cried- Can you tell me what's wrong with me?

Simple, I said calmly. You're not eating properly.

Humor is the most effective and important ingredient, to spice up the dish of our life.

We really do underestimate the most freely available but important aspect in our lives, humor.

Some of us are born lucky if we have a humorous demeanor, others can surely adopt and adapt it and make the 'journey of life' truly enjoyable.

In the **modern world,** life is so hectic and fast that people don't get enough time to relax their mind. As a result, depression, and frustration are common these days.

Humor is one of the best solutions to these kinds of diseases as it is said that a sense of humor is the number one survival skill. It always helps if we maintain a sense of humor even in the midst of adversity.

As a life coach, I have noticed that the goal of counseling is to help people change how they feel and/or how they behave. Counselors use interventions that influence feelings, behaviors and thoughts to help clients feel better and behave differently.

Laughter is an essential part of the human experience. It's true, laughter is strong medicine. It draws people together in ways that trigger healthy physical and emotional changes in the body.

Visiting patients after surgery in various hospitals, I have seen many real life examples of great recovery, when these patients participated in laughter sessions filled with humour, jokes and funny activities

Humour strengthens your immune system, boosts mood, diminishes pain, and protects you from the damaging effects of stress.

Nothing works faster or more dependably to bring your mind and body back into balance than a good humor.

Humor lightens your burdens, inspires hope, connects you to others, and keeps you grounded, focused, and alert. It also helps you release anger and forgive sooner

We all like the environment where everyone is cheerful, smiling and can have a laugh, right? It makes a huge difference.

It creates a safe and supporting environment where people can thrive, feel safe and can bring their true self.

Then why to think more, Start work with a smile on your face; and smile when you attend a meeting.

Have cartoons and pictures near your desk that cheer you up, make you smile or laugh.

Sometimes a picture of someone that is very important to you (e.g. your partner or child, or your pet) can bring an instant smile on your face and let the happy hormones flow.

Share the joy with your parents, spouse, kids and others, a good news story or a small or huge win.

There is nothing better than a clever joke, a witty one liner, some slapstick comedy, or a moment in time sealed with a giggle, chuckle, or side-splitting-laughter.

FOLLOW A HEALTHY LIFESTYLE

"The six best doctors: sunshine, water, rest, air, exercise, and diet."

– *Wayne Fields*

First happiness and a healthy body The proverb may have become old, but even today health remains the first necessity. What is good health? Will a person who is not sick be called a healthy person?

Health is essential and necessary for all. Only a healthy person can do any kind of work smoothly and efficiently.

It is necessary to be healthy in order to lead a happy life. When we are healthy, we can make maximum use of our abilities physically, mentally and socially. By staying healthy, we can lead a happy life.

Being healthy is the main symptom of our health. Only a healthy person can build a healthy and strong nation. In our country, more emphasis is being given on health reforms.

If we turn our eyes around, we will find that we have made a lot of progress. We have everything we used to dream. Today all facilities and needs are at our fingertips.

Technology has given us the knowledge from the earth to the universe. And with this the medical and healthcare industry is also growing rapidly.

A question always comes in my mind that with this technological and materialistic development are we living a healthy life.

Are we able to pay attention to all aspects(physical, mental, emotional, social and spiritual) of our health?

If not,

Then how can we live a healthy and contented life?

As per my experience, I can say that little things matter in our life and by following few small healthy lifestyle tips, we can live a healthy and happy life.

What you gain by living more healthily includes-

Feeling better mentally – regular exercise can lift your mood and help you feel better

Saving money – eating junk food, smoking, and drinking sugary drinks or alcohol are all expensive habits

Fewer health problems – living a healthier lifestyle means a lower risk of developing many illnesses

Taking control of your life – getting healthy helps you feel in control of your life.

Therefore, in order to improve the quality of life, there is a need to give special emphasis on the whole stage in which efficiency, physical stamina, mental satisfaction and happiness are peaceful. An important first step is identifying less healthy habits and learning new, positive ones to replace them, such as:

Eating healthy foods and balanced meals- Eating a wide variety of healthy foods helps to keep you in good health and protects you against chronic disease.

Sleeping well and managing stress- A good night's sleep makes you able to tackle the day's stress more easily. When you're tired, you're less patient and more easily agitated, which can increase stress. Practicing good sleep hygiene along with stress-lowering tactics can help improve your quality of sleep.

Being physically active- Exercise is the miracle cure we've always had, but for too long we've neglected to take our recommended dose. We should all be physically active. It's essential if you want to live a healthy and fulfilling life into old age.

Staying connected with others- Having a network of good relationships improves our wellbeing and can keep your mind active. Staying connected with others and taking part in social activities can also increase your confidence and improve how you feel about yourself.

Being aware of any health risks related to your illness and its treatment, and working with your doctor to monitor these and then take action.

Taking responsibility for your overall health including having regular check-ups for your eyes and teeth.

In order to have a sound mental and emotional state, you must surround yourself with positive energy. Yes, not all problems can be avoided. But it helps to face such obstacles with an optimist outlook.

Surround yourself with encouraging friends and people that will provide you with constructive criticism every once in a while to help you improve.

Make it a habit to always look at the brighter side of life. Even if you find yourself in the worst situation, there is always an upside to it—something good and positive. Dwell on these things instead.

Maintaining a healthy lifestyle is not that difficult, nor does it require a lot of work. Just keep doing what you do and apply the staying healthy tips listed above, surely you will be a well-rounded individual in no time.

Surround Yourself with Positive People

You are the average of the five people you spend the most time with."

– Jim Rohn

Rick and his best friend were both trying to lose weight. They both text each other to check in their progress and whenever Rick is feeling discouraged, his friend would encourage him to continue to work out.

This encouragement helped Rick stay on track with his goal.

Moral of the Story:

Positive people help and support each other grow and not the other way around.

A positive aura enrich your life and make you a happy person.

Positive people follow a fairly simple mantra in life, get rid of the negativity and appreciate the good things in life.

When you're a positive person, you benefit yourself and the ones around you. Surrounding yourself with people who have an optimistic outlook means living a life filled with happy memories.

Positive people not only change your perspective, but also have the power to improve your well-being and overall quality in life.

The person you become is determined by the books you read and the people you surround yourself with. A great mentor told me that early in my career, and it's been the core of my philosophy ever since.

Whenever we feel distressed in our life, then we miss our those friends and loved ones who lifted us up from that despair.

I love spending time with my loved ones, my children and my positive friends, whenever feel stressed and I get energised and excited. My attitude becomes one of confidence and peace.

Be very careful who you surround yourself with, it is your choice who you choose to spend your days with, time is valuable don't waste it engaging in daily consistent failure. Take a look at the people whom you associate with, are they adding value to your life, are these peoples values aligned to yours, do they aspire to reach greater heights in life.

By surrounding yourself with good people, you create good feelings, an atmosphere rich in happiness, you experience blessings after blessings and you prosper because you have a strong support network of people who are good for your mind and soul.

We all have goals in our lives, but which objectives are *musts* in your book? The pursuits you choose to invest time in are a reflection of your standards, and so are your relationships.

All growth starts at the end of your comfort zone. To surround yourself with good people who will take you to the next level, you need to spend time where they are.

greatness is contagious, your life can only improve if you surround yourself with winners.

It's better to hang out with people better than you. Pick out associates whose behaviour is better than yours and you'll drift in that direction." – Warren Buffett

GRATITUDE ROCKS

"Gratitude is the fairest blossom which springs from the soul."

– Henry Ward Beecher

A poor man lived in a village. He was educated, was honest, but kept wandering from door to door for a job. While wandering like this, one day he reached a nearby village and went to a shop and started begging for a job.

Shop-keeper was very experienced. It did not take him long to understand that the man is educated. He gave him a small job in his shop. The man was very happy and started working with Seth with his heart.

Shopkeeper was very impressed with his work and with time he also progressed. Soon the man who wandered from door to door became shopkeeper's accountant.

The qualities were there in him, that is why Seth was very impressed with his work and with time he also progressed.

Soon the man who wandered from door to door became Seth's accountant.

Everything was going well, then Shopkeeper saw that every afternoon the accountant used to lock the doors of his room. Seth began to doubt the accountant. Now Seth started keeping an eye on the bookkeeper everyday. Every afternoon at noon the accountant would lock the door of his room.

One day, as soon as in the afternoon, the accountant stormed the door of his room. Seth reached there and said, open the door.

The accountant opened the door and stood up with folded hands. As soon as he entered the room, Shopkeeper's eyes fell on an old box which was locked. He had doubts, "Certainly, the accountant must have kept the money here.

He forced the bookkeeper to open the box. Shopkeeper was stunned to see the goods lying in the box. In the box were a crushed shirt and a pair of slippers. The accountant said with folded hands, "Sir, these are the same clothes, wearing which I came to your place for the first time to ask for a job.

Looking at these clothes every afternoon, I remember my old days. Today I wear well because of your grace, but everyday I look at these old clothes so that I do not forget the old days and your grace keeps on coming.

We all humans want to be successful in life. In this process of success, the rule of being grateful is the most important. Feeling of thanks towards others.

God has blessed us with many lovely and precious things, parents, family, friends, food, water, air, green trees and loving atmosphere.

We come to know the importance of these things when this thing is not with us, be it food or our guardians. It is only when they are away from us that we come to know their real importance, so in this momentary world, we should have a sense of gratitude for the things around us every day.

We should not forget at all now that there are millions of people who do not get even this much and they struggle day and night only for these things. So forget your sorrows and feel how lucky you are to have these things.

We should always be grateful.

Practice Forgiveness

"Forgiveness is not a feeling; it is a commitment. It is a choice to show mercy, not to hold the offense up against the offender. Forgiveness is an expression of love."

—Gary Chapman

Behavior, feeling and character have great meaning in human life. Forgiveness is considered the ultimate religion in life. Forgiveness and forgiving are words that show utmost simplicity and humility.

It is often said that human beings are the effigy of mistakes, that is, we are human, so we can make mistakes, but we also have the intelligence and discretion to test and understand our mistakes. Sometimes a mistake is made even in the unknown, and sometimes a mistake is made by being careless.

When a man contemplates after his mistake, he finds that he should not have done so, but the mistake made once cannot be rectified, but it can be learned that it should not be repeated in the future.

Forgiveness is a practice I have repeated. Forgiveness is freedom. There is a key that opens the door to healing, happiness and peace, that key is forgiveness. Forgiveness starts from you and it is the greatest gift you can give yourself. Forgiveness of both self and others is the most powerful tool we have.

I have also learned and accepted that the desire for revenge only brings heartache, turmoil and agitation, especially when we have experienced life filled with moments of pains and disappointments.

As a human being, we should accept the fact that making mistakes is a human nature which can happen at any time from oneself or another. Even we ourselves can make mistakes again and again. Therefore, instead of taking someone's mistake to heart, it is great to forgive by showing a big heart.

Forgiving someone not only lightens your mind, but it also has many other health benefits. Let's know about them.

Forgiveness of unpleasant situations, such as a hated job, chronic illness, or the death of a loved one, has been shown to increase stress in people. According to researchers, people who have better ability to forgive, their hearts and minds work better.

Forgiveness can help ease social pain. Social pain is defined as the feeling that comes with social rejection. It often happens when one has a feeling that their life has been spoiled because of people.

The world is responsible for their pain. In such a situation, if you think with a big heart what people have to think, let them think because it is on their mind. If you will not be unhappy with him then you will be able to escape from this social misery.

Forgiveness and depression are intertwined. Self-compassion may moderate the link between a lack of forgiveness and depression. Those people who lacked self-compassion used to be very depressed. If you want to be happy then learn to forgive people.

You should know only one art, that is to forgive people at the right time. By learning to forgive in this way, you can make your life easier with better physical, mental health.

STOP AND SMELL THE ROSES

"There's so much to appreciate about my life every single day, and I make a big point of taking time to smell the roses and noticing how lucky I am. I never want to take that for granted.

—Josie Maran.

Are you feeling overworked?

Are you so concerned with moving up in your career that you feel **stressed** and unhappy?

Do you take time every day to **enjoy the small things in life**?

Most people don't at the time they happen, only in retrospect.

You may naturally feel excited during big life events like weddings, newborn babies, first homes, job promotions, and so on, and I don't mean to diminish their importance.

However, we often reminisce about enjoying the small things in life, those everyday moments that have made up the fabric of our lives.

Feelings of anxiety, sleep difficulties, a compromised immune system, and unexplained aches and pains are not uncommon symptoms of being overly stressed.

Always wanting more instead of enjoying the simple things we already have can lead to a very unsatisfying life.

Kurt Vonnegut said, "**Enjoy the little things in life** because one day you'll look back and realize they were the big things."

The expression "stop and smell the roses" is not just about flowers or nature, but an encouragement to live life with a deeper gratefulness for the world around us.

This is an act of appreciation and recognising the source of the goodness in our lives. It means taking time to recognise the daily moments that bring us joy and really seeing what causes that emotion.

The difference in well-being, happiness, sense of elevation, and level of connectedness to other people, can be significantly higher for those who spend time noticing and savouring these moments of joy.

People who need to stop and enjoy the small things in life should stop working so hard. They need to slow down and take time to **appreciate** the many things that life has to offer. Often this means enjoying the wonders of nature, looking at stars in the night sky, feeling the wind blowing your hair, smelling flowers growing near a busy street.

The thing that you stop to watch could be an old married couple holding hands, a child jumping in a **puddle** or a musician performing by your bus stop. These are the things, simple but beautiful things, that we often walk by in a hurry to get to our next appointment.

It is a reminder to slow down and take notice of the people and events of the day, to be present in every moment, seeing beyond the ordinary and perceive the movement of God.

It means consciously directing your mind to be aware and attentive to the present moment to be able to experience and enjoy more of the world surrounding you.

It means consciously directing your mind to be aware and attentive to the present moment to be able to experience and enjoy more of the world surrounding you. As Mac Davis wisely said:

You gotta stop and smell the roses

You've got to count your many blessings everyday

You're gonna find your way to heaven is a rough and rocky road

If you don't stop and smell the roses along the way.

The ability to appreciate the small things can upgrade your life in a big way. There is reason to celebrate the small things and be grateful every day with just a slight shift in perspective.

Celebrate Life

"Be the celebrators, celebrate! Already there is too much, the flowers have bloomed, the birds are singing, the sun is there in the sky, celebrate it! You are breathing and you are alive and you have consciousness, celebrate it!"

—Osho

The reality is that we live in a fast-paced world. We are taught that "accomplishment" means getting as much done in a day as you possibly can. However, too many of us don't take the time to reflect on our accomplishments. If you struggle with this notion, you aren't alone. Commit to celebrating who you are and loving yourself.

Celebrating is good for people. It's an opportunity for activity, conversation, laughter and excitement with your loved ones and with yourself.

I know you have heard this 1000 times before but I am going to say it again for you. Celebrate every moment in life.

It could be the smallest simplest thing but life itself should be celebrated.

This is the key to the importance of celebrating life. We are social creatures, and we're happier when we connect with each other.

Multiple generations of family come together at birthdays and anniversaries, to think about their shared history, to tell familiar stories and unveil new ones, to enjoy seeing how the children have grown, to feel close to people they've known their whole lives.

Anniversaries remind life partners of the years they've shared, the struggles they've endured, the triumphs they've savoured. Celebrating these events allows people the chance to feel like they've achieved something significant, that their commitment to each other has value in the eyes of their family and friends.

The joy and comfort of these events is an important source of strength for people, even when they may lack the energy to do all the planning themselves.

Celebrations can be easy to postpone or ignore as we get older. Maybe it's hard to think about how many birthdays have passed, or how many anniversaries.

Maybe it's hard to celebrate without worrying about being a burden on family and friends. Maybe there are painful memories or unhealed grief that make celebrating difficult. In all these cases, the answer is to stay focused on the importance of celebrating life.

Finding joy in the gift of life cannot be encapsulated by observing the habits featured in this list–there are pretty much other ways to celebrate life every day.

What matters is that you always manage to wake up and sleep with a grateful heart because you know in yourself that you've been given another chance to be a better version of yourself for your good and the benefit of the people around you.

Don't skip celebrating each and every, big or small event in life, Instead, adjust your plans so that your celebration fits your moods.

JUST DO IT!

If you want to do something, just do it. No one is going to do it for you

—Jamie Pressly

Everyone has a dream to become something in their life and we work hard to follow our dreams. It is very good to have dreams because they help us to choose the correct path and make us successful. It never allows us to waste our time and perform the best.

That's something I've always wanted to do!

These were the exact words that were impulsively uttered by someone I had just met over the weekend at a friend's dinner party.

Isn't it a thing of magic, the way our spirit shines through when we talk about a dream of ours? Or something we truly love? Now imagine how you would feel if you were *actually* pursuing it rather than just talking about it, wouldn't that be something special to experience *at least once* in your lifetime?

So let me ask you this,

What gives you light? What is something you want to make for yourself but are afraid to try?

We both know there's something creative inside of you that you want to bring out and explore.

The biggest injustice you can do for yourself is to sit on the sidelines and wait for the perfect time to arrive—the right time for you to start doing what it is you want to do and create what it is you want to create.

I did this for years upon years, until the day I had a terrible accident; I sustained head injury, tore a knee ligament, and blacked out on the street.

This experience taught me an invaluable lesson in life. Everything you know in your life can be taken away from you at the glance of a moment, so don't waste your life's gift without thinking it through. Instead, live it consciously with courage and gratitude.

Where there is a will there's a way is one of the most used proverbs to date. Its essential meaning is that if you set your mind to do something, you can easily do it. In other words, it shows us the importance of will power and how it can bring a change in someone's life.

Will power is the desire to achieve something. If you have the willpower to do something, then nothing can stop you from doing so. This proverb is equally applicable in almost all aspects of life. Similarly, it holds utmost importance in various ways.

Remember, people who are willing to take the risk, no matter the cost, will successfully achieve their goals. If you just dream and dream about something and do nothing to achieve it, you will most likely fail and become incompetent. On the other hand, if you work continuously to achieve your goals, you can surely find a way.

There's one way to improve your life now....Live It! Don't be afraid of taking a flight, boarding a ship, or riding a train. Live your life as if your life has meaning.

BALANCE THE ELEMENTS OF LIFE

Having the inner strength, balance, and capability to live well irrespective of outside situations and conditions – that is freedom.

Are you someone who takes on more than you should?

Juggling a ton of responsibilities and feeling like you are on the verge of burnout.

You are trying to keep up with every area of your life but you don't know where to start or how to balance it all.

But, balance means something different to everyone.

We all have different lives and responsibilities so what works for one person may not work for another.

Life, in many ways, is a balancing act. Constantly juggling our time between work, home, money, health, relationships, etc. We often fail to understand the importance of having balance in our lives.

Creating balance involves all elements of your life, internal and external. Your internal elements include you, your mind, your heart, your health and your spiritual element. Your external elements are those elements which involve other people and other places. They include your work, social activities, family, and friends.

A well-balanced life must start with a healthy mind and a healthy body. Without either of these things how can we expect to achieve our daily goals and aspirations? If balance is the goal for good health, imbalance is the cause of much suffering and sickness, and unfortunately it's a place where many of us get stuck. Imbalance in your work and home life.

Life is a journey of learning and finding the balance of life. What I would like to share is 7 essential elements of a balanced life.

Internal balance

Mind- Peace and harmony in mind, no negative thoughts, and feelings like anxiety, anger or jealousy, etc.Whenever you do not feel right, try to settle down for yourself to think it over.

Heart- Be open to give and take love. Always remember and be grateful for so much love you get and whenever you have a chance, try to give these love to people who need them. The more you give, the more you get.

Health- Try to keep yourself healthy and improve your immune system function by taking exercise routinely. Only if you are healthy and strong enough, you will be able to have energy, physical strength, and determined will to do what you want to do without excuses, worries, and hesitation.

External Balance

External balance comes from the balance of work & career, financial independence, social relationship, family, fun. Most of the time there are certain and specific things that can be really talked about and visualized. Trying to seek balance among these factors and think about your role and relationship with people around you in a sound and moderate way.

Keep in mind that the balance differs from yours and mine. The priorities change, the goals change or people change, the balance you change. If you want to make it successful, you need to take it more seriously. The more resilient you are, the more instinctively you know how to adjust your behavior. Be open-minded and enjoy it.

ENJOY THE JOURNEY

Life is a journey, and if you fall in love with the journey, you will be in love forever.

– Peter Hagerty

Being happy is for most of us one of the key aims in life. But where we often go wrong is in figuring out which path to take to achieve that happiness.

My own path has been a somewhat unconventional one. Since my last 5 years at journey as a life coach, most of my age group peers were busy spending time staying at home, but I knew that wasn't what I wanted to do.

I wanted to meet the world through my profession, which was met with disapproval by many. But excited, and somewhat scared, I set off alone on my path.

it was a fantastically exciting time and left me with some amazing memories that will last forever.

We often get so caught up chasing after goals or our dreams that we forget that real happiness can be found in the journey. You may think that you will be happy once you get the promotion you have wanted for so long, or you will be happy once you fulfil your lifelong dream of travelling the world.

But the truth is that happiness usually lies in the journey and not just the outcome. With each dream, you have fulfilled or each goal you have accomplished, you may well continue to push the goalpost further and further away or continue to set further goals and work towards additional dreams.

As it turns out, no dream or goal is likely to make us happy forever. You may use your dreams and goals to motivate you, but don't let your dreams get in the way of enjoying the journey of life to the fullest.

Remember that you can give it your best shot but can't always totally control the outcome. So, don't let your happiness depend upon the outcome; try to make the most of the present moments, those that make up your actual life.

Once you do so, you will begin seeing things differently. You would start looking at the journey as an opportunity to learn rather than as a series of challenging landscapes you have to cross for your dreams to come true.

Appreciate what life throws at you because it will allow you to develop and grow stronger. You will stop looking for shortcuts to success and respect the progress you have made so far.

Happy travelling!

CREATE SPACE

"In the never-ending battle between order and chaos, clutter sides with chaos every time. Anything that you possess that does not add to your life or your happiness eventually becomes a burden."

—John Robbins

What are you holding on to that is taking up capacity and making it difficult to create space in your life for what you really want?

Clutter is anything that prevents you from clearing a path or reserving space for what you want or need.

Creating space is a method of opening up your time, energy and physical space to allow more room to live, create and enjoy life. To create physical space, you may need to declutter, change the layout of spaces within your home or office, or even find new places to do the activities that matter to you.

Creating mental space can include removing things or people that drain you of your energy, getting nagging thoughts or ideas out of your head, or having a clear purpose and goals to bring focus to your life.

The key is to make more space in your life, and that starts with these very basic steps- Create space in every way you can, clear out your wardrobe, kitchen cupboards, and desk, everything you can. Why? Because to reconnect, we have to let go of a few things, and physical clutter is a great place to start.

It helps us let go of the past and create space in our lives, room for the universe to send us more of what we ask for.

A quiet, focused mind goes a long way to create space, even when our life and schedule is busy. So does a relaxed, spacious body. In fact, the two go hand in hand and are deeply interconnected.

I've found that the exercise of writing things down already creates a greater awareness of my actions. I am more likely to choose healthier food to eat if I know I'm having to write it down. The same is true of tracking time.

We've become so used to the high priority placed on cell phones that it's easy to ignore how they've begun taking over our lives and our time. The act of simply tracking how much time you spend on your phone per day can be frightening.

The whole intent behind decluttering is to create more space in your home and your life. Declutter items from your home so that you can spend less time cleaning and picking up and more time invested with your family and on other things you care about.

Likewise, as you declutter your schedule from perceived obligations and additional activities, you have now freed yourself up to do more of what is important to you. You've created time and space to focus on other goals which could include relaxing and enjoying life at home with your family.

When you create boundaries with technology and limit the amount of time you are willing to spend on your phone, computer, and television, a whole new world opens up for you. Imagine the number of books you could read or additional time you could be sleeping.

Do you have goals you would like to accomplish? Decluttering should be part of your goals to make space in your life to work on those dreams. It will likely require some sacrifices and changes in habits, but the pay off will be worth it.

Support Yourself With Loving Thoughts

"A person learns how to love himself through the simple acts of loving and being loved by someone else."

—Haruki Murakami

For most of my 30's, I had a very poor relationship with myself. I was always striving for external satisfaction whilst my inner dialogue was judgmental, critical, and negative. I never felt like I was good enough or worthy. The truth is, I didn't even know who I was under all the layers of guilt, expectation, and anxiety I had built up around me.

Is this happening to you too?

Do you tear yourself down and criticise yourself with your thoughts?

What if you were to instead empower and support yourself?

What if you were to back yourself, uplift yourself and choose to love yourself deeply.

So many of us go through life disconnected from our inner self, looking for something else (or someone else) to complete us. When we draw our awareness deeper inwards, we begin to feel supported, guided, and at peace. Like any relationship, the one we have with ourself requires time and commitment to build.

To know yourself is to love yourself, and to love yourself is everything.

There's no relationship more important than the one you have with yourself.

Self-love means that you accept yourself fully, treat yourself with kindness and respect, and nurture your growth and wellbeing.

Self-love encompasses not only how you treat yourself, but your thoughts and feelings about yourself. So, when you conceptualise self-love, you can try to imagine what you would do for yourself, how you would talk to yourself, and how you would feel about yourself that reflects love and concern.

Practice self-love include:

People who have more self-love tend to know what they think, feel, and want.

By staying focused on what you need, you turn away from automatic behaviour patterns that get you into trouble, keep you stuck in the past, and lessen self-love.

You will love yourself more when you take better care of your basic needs. People high in self-love nourish themselves daily through healthy activities, like sound nutrition, exercise, proper sleep, intimacy and healthy social interactions.

I write down my accomplishments. I love this self-love

activity because it creates a record of your accomplishments (big and small) that you can re-read whenever you're feeling low. Add to it and read your list on a daily basis for maximum benefit.

Don't shy away from uncomfortable feelings like anger and sadness. If you deny them, you deny a part of yourself. Allow yourself to express them in a healthy, respectful way.

Finally, to practice self-love, start by being kind, patient, gentle and compassionate to yourself, the way you would with someone else that you care about.

EXPLORE YOUR SPIRITUALITY

"Your sacred space is where you can find yourself over and over again."

— Joseph Campbell

Science is a very valuable part of humanity. However, it hasn't yet explained it all. Stepping fully into a meaningful life requires a shift in the way we show up for ourselves and others.

Spirituality is the broad concept of a belief in something beyond the self.

First, one must understand the true meaning of spirituality. Many of us consider ourselves to be spiritual when in reality, we are religious. We pray to a God, we follow our religion, we practice rituals prescribed by it and we think this is spirituality. But spirituality is beyond religion. Religion is only the kindergarten of spirituality.

We live with superstitions and myths. Because all of us have been conditioned and taught to believe in theology based on our scriptures.

Most of us are confused about what a spiritual life is. Being spiritual doesn't mean we become a hermit and live an ascetic life in a forest. Or we wear saffron robes and a rosary. A spiritual life is about realizing the Spirit, our true self. It is awakening to the truth about who we are.

I believe, being spiritual is how you see yourself in relation to your friends, your family and your world.

Here I'm going to share a real life story of a villager, who inspired lots of people including me with his great values, learnings and experiences. Let's read

In a small village, lived a man who was always happy, kind, and well disposed to everyone he met.

This man always smiled, and had kind and encouraging words to say.. Everyone who met him, left feeling better, happier and elated. People knew they could count on him, and regarded him as a great friend.

One of the village dwellers was curious to know what his secret was, and how he could always be so kind and helpful. He wondered, how is it that he held no grudge toward anyone, and always was happy.

Once, upon meeting him he asked him: "Most people are selfish and unsatisfied. They do not smile as often as you do; neither are they as helpful or kind as you are. How do you explain it?"

The man smiled at him and replied, "When you make peace with yourself, you can be in peace with the rest of the world.

If you can recognise the inner soul in yourself, you can recognise the spirit in everyone, and then you will find it natural to be kind and well disposed to all

The mind is like a robot programmed to do certain tasks. Habits and thoughts are the tools and programs that control the mind. You need to free yourself from this programming. Then, the inner good and the happiness that reside within you will be revealed."

"But a lot of work is necessary. Good habits have to be developed. The ability to focus and to control thoughts has to be strengthened.

The work is difficult and endless. There are many fences that need to be climbed. It is not an easy task."

"Do not think about the difficulties, otherwise, this is what you will see and experience. Just make your feelings and thoughts quiet, and try to stay in this peace. Just try to be calm, and do not let yourself be carried away by your thoughts."

"Is that all?" Asked the villager.

"Try to watch your thoughts and see how they come and go and stay in the silence that arises.

The moments of peace will be brief at first, but in time, they will get longer. This peace is also strength, power, kindness, and love.

In time, you will realize that you are one with the Universal Power, and this will lead you to act from a different dimension, different point of view and different consciousness, not from the selfish, small, limited ego."

"I will try to remember your words," said the villager, and continued, "there is another thing that I am curious about. You do not seem to be influenced by the environment. You always seem to be happy. You always have a kind word for everyone, and you are helpful. People treat you well, and never exploit your goodness."

"Some people think that being good and being kind means weakness. The truth is that they mean inner strength, and do not point to weakness.

When you are kind and empathetic, you can also be strong.

People sense your inner strength, and therefore, do not impose on you. When you are strong and calm inside, you help people, because you can, and you want to. You act from strength, not from weakness.

Goodness is not a sign of weakness. A good character can manifest together with power and strength.

When you are calm inside, you are also happy. When your mind is quiet, there is no anger, no resentment and no negative thoughts. This leads to happiness and to a feeling of content and joy."

"Thank you very much for your advice and explanations", said the villager, and went away happy and satisfied.

We all have the power to focus our thoughts in a positive direction, positive for ourselves, for others, and for the world. Dedicating the first 10 minutes of each day just to being still and connecting with something greater than yourself is a way to do just that.

Give it a try and start practicing meditation or yoga, reading an inspirational text, or taking a walk in nature right upon waking.

Obsessing over our personal wants and desires creates isolation, not happiness. Instead, practice simple ways to be of service to others: Offer your seat on public transport to someone who needs it more than you, smile at the person preparing your coffee, listen to others without judgment.

Always remain yourself. You are your own unique and glorious flavour and contribution to this world. That is what spirituality is meant to help you discover too.

It is the spirituality that helps us attain the ultimate goal of human life to realise we are the Divine Soul. This is the secret to living a life of peace and bliss.

Get into Nature

"In every walk with nature, one receives far more than he seeks."

– John Muir

Sitting on a beach. Listening the sound of waves. Laying in the grass doing nothing. Taking in a breathtaking view from the top of a mountain.Yea, right. Who has time for that?

This is my own experience, that in today's digital age, when we cannot even imagine our life without technology. But still we cannot deny the benefits of nature. Recent studies suggest that nature can help our brains and bodies to stay healthy.

We all are living a busy life locked away in an office, work place or at home far away from nature. Yearly vacation can't come fast enough. Right now we are stressed. We want to recharge, relax, and experience peace, just for a little bit.

Did you know that you can get closer to nature and recharge your body without traveling far or taking too much time off of your busy schedule?

Whenever I feel physical and mental stress due to high work pressure.

I go to the park, and soon I feel stress free with the touch of fresh air. Blooming flowers, flying butterflies, the sound of birds always has a calming effect and takes me out of my own head.

It helps to keep me calm and physically healthy, and I love taking the time to be mindful of all the beautiful green spaces around me, even when living in a city.

So whenever you feel any kind of stress, or fatigue, then visit a nearby park.You can read a book by sitting under any tree, and enjoy the benefits of fresh air and natural colours.

Being close to nature seems like a no-brainer. It's been long associated with being healthy, stress-free, mindful and meditative. The scientific community has recently become interested in the power of nature and has discovered many benefits of being close to our natural environment.

Spending time in nature and being close to things that come from nature, including indoor plants, herbs, crystals, and stones can promote vitality.

But don't forget. Be kind with Mother Nature. Recycle, eat organic fruits and vegetables, don't litter and don't waste water. Turn off lights when you're not using them. Don't hurt animals or plants. Consider becoming a vegetarian or vegan.

To truly connect to nature, you need to go outside and experience it for yourself!

MAKE TIME FOR WHAT YOU LOVE

"Believe in yourself, listen to your gut, and do what you love."

—Dylan Lauren

About a year ago, I realized I wasn't spending enough time doing the things I love, giving enough time for social interactions, surfing, and traveling. Life started to feel lousy.

I sometimes wonder why we get voluntarily overwhelmed by the things that don't even matter.

Don't underestimate the importance of making time doing things you love. Time flies. It's easy to think that "tomorrow" will be a better day to do things that will lead to a better life.

Do what you love today, singing, dancing, writing, playing, traveling, whatever brings your energy and happiness back.

Make time for the things that make you happy and for people you love. Time flies and you don't want to look back one day with regret.

I believe we should set our direction, Otherwise, someone else will do it for you. Figure out where you are going and then work on the way to get there.

It's okay not to know all the answers now. Be patient and take it little by little, step by step. The journey will uncover.

The worst thing is to not take any action. Staying still will slowly kill you.

Once you love something, you don't care how much time or energy you invested in it. It brings you joy. And this is what it's all about.

I have noticed that small joys bring tremendous happiness in our life. I recommend that Stop and celebrate silly things other than birthdays and anniversaries. Find a reason to buy balloons and a cake and invite some friends to celebrate a little milestone in your life.

I love listening to music, be it classical, contemporary, jazz or rap. It gives me serenity. And I feel like all my tiredness, stress and pain is gone. Listen to some music that you enjoy. Music is a great therapy.

Sometimes, we take the people we love for granted. Look around at the people in your life and show them that you love them.

Take the time to move your body. It doesn't have to be a full exercise regimen. Just put on some music and move around. Every part of you that can move, move it! It heals the mind and the body when you take the time your physical body needs in movement.I love it

I have realized that most of our productivity are going in vain , just because of overuse of technology and screens. Take tech free time, even if only for an hour a day, frees your mind and helps you realize that you can have 'time off' every day. Try it and see how it feels.

This may seem like a long list, yet if you pick a few that you know won't take much time and go for it, your life energy will shift. You get so busy, and there seems to be this big rush to the finish line. Just remember that on the way to the finish line there is a beautiful view.

Don't miss it.

GET BACK TO YOUR BASICS

"When knowledge becomes overwhelming, go back to the basics"

—Author: Abdulkadir Abdullahi Mohamed Mirre

When I ask millennials, "What would be a successful life for you?" the responses range from being wealthy, being a top executive in their company, being famous and known, to setting up their own business, traveling the world, and so on.

However, when I ask, "What is it that gives you lasting happiness?" I get very different responses: "Making my family happy, helping people in need, being in love, being understood and valued, enjoying quality time with friends."

It all boils down to devouring the simple joys in life and having fulfilling relationships.

Initially, I found it strange to see that people have different paths to success and happiness. Can't success make you happy? And isn't being happy, being successful?

As I continued to delve deeper into those powerful questions, I realized that our definition of success is largely shaped by society. You are successful only if you are rich, popular, at the top of the corporate ladder with a huge mansion.

The other day as I was having a meeting with one of my clients in a cafe, I could overhear a bunch of ten something sitting on the next table discussing how tough the work environment is. How bosses don't trust you.

They were trying to call the waiter but as it was a busy time, it took a while for their waiter and food to come. the waiter finally came with their food. One of them burst out and complained about the delay, in a rather rude way. The waiter apologized and called the manager who did the same.

With no intention of judging anyone, I was astounded at the sheer dichotomy of words and actions, causing them to shout and complain about their work environment for the exact same behaviour of impatience and intolerance, which they were guilty of themselves, in another work environment, without even realizing it.

If we want to live a simpler, happier life, we need to go back to basics and rekindle the values of empathy, tolerance, compassion, trust and love in ourselves.

Easier said than done? Sure - but here are few tips to help simplify your life

Identify the things that add unnecessary complexity, busyness, and overwhelm to your life and work. Create a plan to reduce, eliminate, or manage those things.

Get clear on the things that make the most difference and create the most benefit to achieving what matters most to you. Create a plan to do more of those things. Make them habits.

Put boundaries in place to protect them.

Simplify everything. Simplicity is the antidote to complexity, busyness, and overwhelm. Become a master of simplifying. It is a superpower in the quest to achieve consistent and predictable results effectively.

We all spend a lot of our time, attention, and focus every day, week, month, and year on things that don't really matter at the cost of what does. That has a negative impact on progress, achieving what matters most to you, etc. You can change that by creating and implementing a back to basics strategy.

Enjoy life's simple pleasures. They're free and better than anything money can buy.

Really listen to others

"Listening is a magnetic and strange thing, a creative force. The friends who listen to us are the ones we move toward. When we are listened to, it creates us, makes us unfold and expand."

— Karl A. Menniger, psychiatrist

In my experience as a therapist, I can say that good listening skills play a vital role in today's world. Listening is more than just hearing, however.

Just because a person acts like they hear a message does not necessarily mean that they really "heard" you.

One of the key ways to reduce family or workplace conflict and to improve family communication is to polish our listening skills. When we listen well to other people, we encourage them to talk about what is most important to them. It's all too easy to be careless about really listening in families.

To truly listen, you must give your undivided attention and put your own agenda and needs aside.

Sometimes we assume that we know what the other person means or we pretend to listen while we do something else. If you were only half-listening, not making eye contact, or glancing at your phone, the other person won't want to waste their breath. They won't trust you to respect their thoughts and feelings.

It happened with me several ties, when due to not paying attention to what a loved one is trying to convey, many relationship got bitter.

Then In started listening carefully and gained all the relations back.

So pay attention and put aside what you are doing when someone wants to share his/her feelings or messages with you.

Listening strengthens relationships and demonstrates attentiveness, caring, and respect. When we listen, we encourage others to talk about what is important to them.

Humans are naturally empathetic, but we all have biases and assumptions that come from our upbringing and experiences.

When you talk to people who have different backgrounds and experiences, it can be tempting to lean on preconceived notions. Instead, you can commit to listening rather than assuming.

When you hear right from a source, you'll have a deeper understanding of their perspective, which is key to having empathy.

Communication is key in most aspects of life, whether that be with friends, family, work colleague or partners. A lot of issues can be created or avoided through it. So use this method wisely.

NO REGRET

"Accept everything about yourself – I mean everything, You are you and that is the beginning and the end – no apologies, no regrets."

—Henry A. Kissinger

When you look back on your life, how do you feel? How will you feel in another 15 years? Will you be sitting on your porch in your rocking chair reminiscing about all you've accomplished — or thinking about your regrets?

No one wants to reach the end of their life and not have achieved everything they wanted. No one wants to have "if only's" and "what ifs

To live life without regrets doesn't mean you never make a mistake. It doesn't mean you never fail. It means that you live life to the fullest and learn from your experiences.

We all have things we regret doing or things we regret not doing.

We stay in unfulfilling jobs and unhealthy relationships. We pass up opportunities out of fear or uncertainty. Yet regret can also be a powerful driver for change.

When you shift your view from "living my life with no regrets" to "living an authentic, purposeful life," you'll discover endless opportunities for personal growth.

Do what you love. Life is too short to waste your time doing things that don't make you happy. Spend your time with your loved ones, find a fulfilling hobby, and give back through volunteering.

Learning how to live life without regret can be difficult. You may feel set in your ways, but being open to new experiences is essential.

Get out of your comfort zone. Comfort is the best friend of regret. Seek out new experiences. It's never too late to overcome your fears.

Everyone wants to live life without regrets and can. All you have to do is live boldly and dare to be your authentic self.

Use these strategies to help ensure that when you reach the end of your life, you can be confident you did everything you could to make the most of it.

Tap your creative self

"A creative life is an amplified life. It's a bigger life, a happier life, an expanded life, and a hell of a lot more interesting life"

— Elizabeth Gilbert

My teenage daughter, who is interested in psychology, asked me recently: "Mom, what is the one thing that you can't live without?"

I immediately thought Love. And I think that is probably true.

I shared my thoughts with her. She responded, "That's great mom. You have love, so now what? What is the most important thing? What do you most want to do with your days and with your life?"

It got me thinking about how I best like to spend my days and the kind of work I do. I am happiest when I feel challenged and creative. If I had a mundane job doing the same thing eight hours a day to get a pay check, I wouldn't be happy.

Creativity is the drive and energy behind my best-spent days and most successful endeavors.

I am at my best when I am writing daily something on a new topic and I am cooking, my fingers tapping happily at the keyboard or literally cooking in the kitchen. The most important thing I want to do in my life, is getting connected and providing support and care to people who are in need.

Creativity can be anything that has meaning to you, which means there can be creativity in nearly everything you do, study, relationships, travel, customer service, even cleaning!

If it has meaning to you, if it brings you joy, satisfaction, or a sense of accomplishment, it can be your special creative outlet.

Research shows that having a creative hobby can boost brain activity, help individuals cope with stress and promote overall wellness and positivity.

If it has meaning to you, if it brings you joy, satisfaction, or a sense of accomplishment, it can be your special creative outlet.

Research shows that having a creative hobby can boost brain activity, help individuals cope with stress and promote overall wellness and positivity.

In order to pinpoint your unique creative outlet, try asking yourself these starter questions:

What gives me meaning?

What brings me joy?

What makes me unique?

What do my friends love about me?

What do I daydream about?

Some of your answers might be cooking, gardening, being a great listener, making people smile, being a really organized person. Believe it or not, all of these things are creative endeavours. All it takes is first recognising it's *your* art and your form of expression.

Now that you know your creative self, it's time to think of it as your masterpiece and of yourself as an artist. As an artist, it's important to acknowledge the ways in which you excel at your craft.

Once you've taken ownership of your creativity, the magic can begin. Creativity becomes even more powerful when you think outside of the box and explore new ways to express your talent.

When you give yourself permission to call yourself a creative and believe it, a whole world of innovative thinking, self-expression, and joy will open up to you.

Anyone can unlock their creative potential. For most, increasing imagination, inspiration, and originality are as simple as learning a few new techniques.

Then why thinking, tap your creativity and enter into the new artistic world with ultimate new imaginations and opportunities.

Never Stop, Keep Improving

"Continuous improvement is better than delayed perfection".

– Mark Twain

I believe *Self-improvement is the turnkey tip that helps you achieve your goals. One of the best things about life is that we never have to stop improving.*

As a passionate advocate of growth, I'm also continuously looking for ways to self-improve. I've been reading plenty of short stories on self improvement in the past couple of weeks and found the lessons behind them truly wonderful. So I've decided to share one of them.

As a group of frogs was traveling through the woods, two of them fell into a deep pit. When the other frogs crowded around the pit and saw how deep it was, they told the two frogs that there was no hope left for them.

However, the two frogs decided to ignore what the others were saying and they proceeded to **try and jump out of the pit**.

Despite their efforts, the group of frogs at the top of the pit were still saying that they should just give up. That they would never make it out.

Eventually, one of the frogs took heed to what the others were saying and he gave up, falling down to his death. The other frog continued to jump as hard as he could. Again, the crowd of frogs yelled at him to stop the pain and just die.

He jumped even harder and finally made it out. When he got out, the other frogs said, **"Did you not hear us?"**

The frog explained to them that he was deaf. He thought they were encouraging him the entire time.

Moral of the story:

People's words can have a big effect on other's lives. Think about what you say before it comes out of your mouth. It might just be the difference between life and death.

Ever since we were young, we were told to excel in academics, focus on getting good grades and ace our exams. In schools and colleges, the learning has always been more directed towards academics, but what about aspects like self-improvement and personal development that play an equally important role in people's lives?

The importance of self-improvement often goes unnoticed. We are either conveniently brushing our shortcomings under the carpet, refusing to face them or are just happy being ignorant.

The main reason why we stop improving is, we stop learning new things, we stop purposefully practicing, we stop believing, we stop trying.

Even after a single failure we easily give up on things.

Practicing is the best way of improving. If we check history, even greatest talents are really the results of years of practice. Great personalities faced thousands of unsuccessful attempts before they created something unbelievable. They didn't give up on his first failure, he kept believing, he kept trying.

A common growing obstacle often we face is after reaching a particular skill level that we feel 'satisfactory', we stop improving, we practice it daily still we are not moving ahead, we get stuck in these automated performance repetitions.

Then how to get out of them?

We spend so much time getting to know other people and solve their issues. If only we spent that much time knowing ourselves, things would have been so much more different. Isn't it?

So, in order to be on the path of self-improvement, it is important to never lose touch with yourself.

From relationships to careers, knowing your strengths is important for every sphere of your life.

By nurturing and playing on your strengths, you are more likely to attain success and move towards shaping a happier and more productive life.

Challenges and obstacles are the part of success and growth. Choosing to work on improving yourself requires you to step out of your comfort zone. It lets you face your fears, try new things, take risks and challenge yourself.

Last but not the least, self-improvement cultivates self love and compassion. By seeing yourself grow with every passing day, you build on your confidence and self-esteem.

So, whether you are a retired 60 year old or a 25 year old who is just starting off his/her career, remember that you will always be work in progress and there can never be an end to learning about yourself. That is what makes life purposeful and fun.

(Keep growing and have fun:)

Be Emotionally Intelligent

"We are stronger than we think. We have emotional, spiritual and even physical resources at our disposal. We may get knocked down, but we don't have to stay down."

—Steve Goodier

The great greek philosopher Aristotle described what it means to be emotionally intelligent hundreds of years before the term became popular.

He said: *"Anyone can become angry, that is easy. But to be angry with the right person, to the right degree, at the right time, for the right purpose, and in the right way, that is not easy."*

What's important to note is that the way we take of ourselves physically 100% impacts how we feel emotionally.

Think about it...

When you don't eat, you get cranky.

When you get poor sleep, you're more easily irritated.

Let's start with the meaning of emotional balance – When we face unpleasant situations we automatically react with anger, worry, fear, anxiety etc.

Having emotional balance helps us to attain flexibility and promotes stabilisation between our mind and body.

In other words emotional balance teaches us how to respond to negative emotions and thoughts without just getting stuck in them.

It is important to know and apply this in order to increase your quality of sleep, concentration, conscious, motivation and happiness.

Focus on what you exactly feel and how it affects your body. It could be helpful to close your eyes and try to figure out which body part you feel tension.

Describe the emotion with words. Be ready to say "I'm anxious.", "I'm feeling sad." This helps you to take a step back from your automatic reaction and respond more consciously.

Regulate and recognise your emotions and take necessary action to deal with the situation

For example, lessen the tension of an emotion by engaging in activities like meditation, yoga and breathing exercises etc.

Life does not just consist of happy and joyful moments, there are also some sad, fearful and painful situations.

The important part is to know how you can handle these negative events and how not to allow them to affect your emotions.

So, remember to balance your unhappy emotions, when you feel stressed and take life as it comes and enjoy the ride!!

GET RID OF THINGS THAT ARE WEIGHING YOU DOWN

"If you want to fly, you have to give the things that weigh you down."

I was outside recently doing a bit of gardening work, when I noticed a tree in front. The tree's limbs were hanging very close to the ground and it was weighing the tree down. Ironically, I hadn't noticed this previously.

I got my clippers out and began to cut the tree limbs. I found it fascinating to watch how the tree began to spring up after each limb that I cut as if a heavy burden had been lifted. When I finished cutting the tree it looked different, lighter, almost happier, which got me thinking. In life (and business) there are many things that can weigh us down, mentally, physically and emotionally.

One of my friends told me this story to inspire me to move on.

There lived a man, he wanted to climb the highest mountain in the world. After many years of preparation he decided to give it a go.

Because he wanted to achieve glory alone, he started climbing the mountain alone.

It was cold, the night arrived, it was dark, zero visibility but he still wanted to climb. Instead of taking a halt, he kept climbing.

Suddenly, his foot slipped and he lost his control. It was a free fall, he felt the pull of gravity. In those moments of great fear, it reminded of all the good and bad things he did in his life.

He was now thinking of how close was his death, all of a sudden he felt a hard pull by a rope tied to his waist.

His body was now hanging, with only a support of rope, He cried and screamed, "***Help me God.*** ".

A voice came from the cloud, "***What do you want me to do?***"

The man cried, "***Save me God!***"

The voice came, "***Will you do as I say?***"

The man cried, "***Yes, anything, Please save me.***"

The voice came, "***Cut the rope tied on your waist.***"

The man did not cut the rope and held it with all his strength.

Next morning when the rescue team arrived, it said that the climber was dead and frozen, he was holding on his rope which was frozen,

Only six feet above ground!

So, how attached are you with your rope? Will you let go?

Most people I know are carrying extra weight, and I'm not talking about gaining a few pounds.

I'm talking about the mental and emotional weight we lug around with us. We carry it everywhere,

Personally, much of my extra weight comes from the expectations I have for myself to be more, more present, more productive, more enlightened.

Although these might be wonderful things to work toward, wanting to be *more* can easily translate to not being enough *now*.

For me it happens to be expectations, but our habits can weigh us down too. Watching television that doesn't nourish our souls, eating foods that don't nourish our bodies, and holding on to thoughts that don't nourish our minds. The effects add up.

To be able to enjoy life to the fullest, you've got to have ample room for the things that matter most, those that bring you joy.

This means ditching the things that are only a drain on you. Dump all the judgments, limiting beliefs, painful memories, unchecked thoughts, harmful habits, or denied emotions are in your backpack.

Relish in the positive relationships and relaxing living space you've curated for yourself. You deserve it!

DEEPEN YOUR CONNECTIONS WITH OTHERS

"Connecting with others gives us a sense of inclusion, connection, interaction, safety, and community. Your vibe attracts your tribe, so if you want to attract positive and healthy relationships, be one! Staying connected and getting reconnected feeds the flow of goodness which empowers our humanity."

—Susan C. Young

I had written an article post about loneliness for my social media handles, not to long ago and since then I have been going out and getting myself out there, trying to get out of this loneliness funk.

Because I too get lonely.

It got me thinking about how people deal with loneliness, why people feel this way, and how to get over it.

One of the main reasons why people get lonely is because

they feel disconnected. And to overcome this, the obvious answer would be…well to connect.

However, in order to start connecting with people at least one person needs to initiate that connection and if the other person doesn't, we must decide for ourselves whether take it into our own hands to start.

Have you ever walked down a familiar street or walkway?

And instead of saying "Hi" to the person walking past you, you look down or look ahead, making it look like they didn't exist?

Or making it look like you are busy?

It's okay, I've done this to…maybe too many times.

Acknowledging people's existence is the first step in connecting with people. Just start saying "Hi" to people and you will set the tone.

Yes, there is a chance they will ignore you.

Yes, there is a chance they walk right past you.

Yes, there is a chance they may just say "Hi" back.

Yes, there is a chance where they may respond by asking how your day went.

Yes, there is a chance you may surprise them for acknowledging their existence.

Yes, they may even start engaging with you.

No matter what the outcome is, start saying "Hi" to people even if they don't look like the type to reciprocate.

Don't you feel special when someone remembers your name instead of saying "Hey You!"?

Learning a person's name is like gold when it comes to connecting people. Make an effort to know a person's name regardless if they know yours.

Compliments are FREE.

I was shopping at a Lifestyle store the other day and when I went to the cashier to pay for my cloths, the lady scanning my things had such a kind gesture and lovely voice. It was very respectful and calm.

Well, I told her that she had an excellent kind gesture and she was taken aback. One, she had never heard that compliment, she wasn't expecting it.

She told me, with the biggest smile, that with that compliment I had made her day and of course she made mine.

In fact, I feel like everyone should give more compliments to each other, when necessary.

We all need and crave connection but sometimes we need to take it into our own hands to initiate it.

Scroll less, live more

> *"The reason why we struggle with insecurity is because we compare our behind the scenes with everyone else's highlight reel."*
>
> —Steven Furtick

Can we imagine our life without technology, social media and screens today?

Sure, short videos are entertaining as hell (even if I feel way too uncool for some of the dances), and Instagram gave us true blessings like avocado toast, whipped coffee, and Jennifer Aniston breaking the internet.

Social media is an effortless way to stay connected to loved ones, network in your field, and keep up with the latest from favourite brands, celebs, and publications.

However, too much social media can take up your time, distract you from being productive, and might even make you unhappy.

I myself experienced many negative consequences of technology's wrong use, and then decided to follow a few rules to avoid the wrong and over use of it.

I started tracking my time online. Once you have observed the areas that need to be rectified and defined your goal time for everyday usage, apps like Facebook and Instagram offer a screen limit reminder that can be activated to keep you on track.

The second thing you should start doing, avoid checking your phone the first thing in the morning.

And If social media has been eating your quality time with your loved ones, a good place to begin rectifying that would be to opt for device-free meals so you can reconnect with everyone and catch up on their day.

The easiest way to reduce our dependence on our phones is to replace virtual conversations with in person conversation.

I hope these self made rules may encourage you to learn how to spend less time on social media so you can focus on growing your personal and professional life.

Try New Things

"Life is about taking chances, trying new things, having fun, making mistakes and learning from it."

—Anonymous

Have you ever been scared to try something new?

It's an understandable fear and one that I relate to keenly. However, I've recently begun to look at trying new things in a different way and realized that new experiences can bring us incredible benefits.

I'm not asking you to climb Kilimanjaro or make a drastic change in your career. All I'm saying is that you and I should dabble occasionally in new and different hobbies that peak our interest out of our comfort zone.

Growth will naturally happen when you do things you haven't done before because it causes you to be more aware of your situation. It provides incredible benefits to your mental health. Take courage to do something new without fear.

Let me distract you for a moment and tell you a short story.

This is an old story, a familiar one.

I hope the twist we've put on here inspires you to think differently.

Once there was a king who was curious but wealthy. He decided to test his fellow people to know who has a good attitude in life and who would spare some time for the country's progress.

He placed a huge boulder right at the middle of the road and hid in a nearby place to see if anyone would make an attempt to move it off.

He saw some wealthy merchants and courtiers passing by the road. None of them made any attempt to move it off but simply walked away while some others blamed the king for not maintaining roads.

Later, a peasant came the way with a load of vegetables and saw the boulder. He kept his load down and tried to move the boulder away. After strenuous effort, he succeeded in moving it away. He saw a purse lying in the place of the boulder.

It contained many gold coins and a note from the king which read 'this is the reward for the person who moves the boulder away.

Moral: It is quite common for people to run away from problems and obstacles. But the story clearly shows the importance of seeing an opportunity in every obstacle which might improve our condition. Invest some time to remove obstacles on your way and experience many unseen presences.

Essentially, by trying new things, you benefit from new and special memories that will last a lifetime.

What if the next new thing you try is the passion of your life?

The more you try, the more you'll learn about your likes and dislikes, because they're unique to you.

One of the best and most exciting benefits of trying new things is that you overcome fear. It might sound too good to be true, but the reality is that fear is simply our reaction to the unknown.

Our biggest benefit of trying new things is that it *actually* increases your creative capacity. Every single time you put yourself in a new situation, you force your brain to quickly understand a unique set of circumstances,

So, if you're trying gardening for the first time, your brain is working in a new unique way. Even if gardening is old news for you, try anything for the first time, there's a unique set of rules and so your brain will use its creativity to find a way to succeed.

The benefits of trying new things are incredible, and there's no reason to wait! Start now with something new.

NURTURE YOUR INNER CHILD

"No one's going back for that inner child. Except you."

—Tanya Markul

Everyone has an inner child.

The inner child is the part of ourselves that still retains its innocence, creativity, awe, and wonder toward life. Quite literally, your inner child is the child that lives within you.

Too often we reach adulthood and forget to see through those childlike eyes again.

We might have suffered as children and we cannot remember any such experiences at all. But I can assure you, the child you were, found them in moments where they could, because this is the child's gift.

Children have an innate capacity to find the tiny places of beauty, even in the midst of great darkness. Children create fantastical worlds in their imagination which take them away from the present and into another richer and more colorful place.

What we often fail to see as adults is that this child part of ourselves is usually still present, even when we have been wounded as children and are still wounded.

When we ignore it, this part of ourselves makes itself known in ways which can cause us problems. The wounded inner child often manifests itself in self-destructive or self-sabotaging behaviours.

Some of the behaviours we might see are self-harming and addictions like overeating, using drugs or alcohol, overspending and gambling. We could also find ourselves overreacting emotionally or experiencing conflict in a lot of our relationships.

Inner Child work requests presence and pause, and turning into our darkness and perhaps staying there for a bit.

A relationship with your inner child is like any other kind of relationship. When we begin inner child healing work, we tap into a part of ourselves that is vulnerable and impressionable. We're able to be both the "grown-up" and the child, providing unconditional self-love, self-compassion, and self-support.

We can't go back and change the past, but we can loosen the grip the past has on us. Here are some ways that you can start the healing process through listening to your pain and triggers, talking to your loved ones, remembering how to play and through creativity.

Inner child work has important emotional benefits, but it can also make a big difference in your relationships and your work.

LET GO OF COMPARISON

"No one can make you feel inferior without your consent."

— Eleanor Rosevelt

Human beings are social creatures and comparison is common throughout our entire history.

Sometimes these comparisons can be helpful. They can give you a blueprint for improvement and inspire you to change. Other times, they can be a means to pick yourself apart and see everything that you think is wrong with yourself.

Comparing yourself to others is something that stops you from accepting yourself and healing your soul.

Letting go of comparison might sound impossible which is why, at this point I'm sharing a few tips that can serve as a guide. These tips will help you to **stop comparing yourself to others** and heal yourself.

As per my personal experiences, I can mention here that too much use of technology and social media, we are in the trap of fake comparisons of look, material shows etc.

Too much comparison leads to unhappiness and low self esteem. We become frustrated with ourselves for not being good enough, or angry with others.

Feelings of jealousy, frustration, and hopelessness emerge if comparisons continue. If left unaddressed, chronic anxiety and depression can stem from such behaviour.

To stop the comparison habit, focus on bettering yourself and boosting your confidence. Try to train your mind to stay away from unfavorable comparisons.

Seek instead to embrace kindness and a positive attitude. It's hard work, but it pays off.

Though it's impossible to ignore when someone else is better at something than you are, there are always things that you are good at as well.

You need to start concentrating on your strengths to avoid comparison.

To **stop comparing yourself to others**, start writing down things you like about yourself. Being aware of your strengths enables you to be more confident so you can work on healing your soul.

The only person you should be comparing yourself to is yourself. Your efforts should focus on growing from within, being kinder, more resilient, working hard, and being more open instead of whether or not your hair is long enough or you're as strong as someone else.

No one truly knows what's happening behind the scenes in someone else's life. Being inspired by someone you know to be kinder or more open-minded can lead you to be a better person.

You are already doing your best and it's about time that you start giving yourself some credit from where you are in life.

Rather than **comparing yourself to others,** express gratitude to yourself for the life you've created.

SET HEALTHY BOUNDARIES WITH OTHERS

"We need to have a talk on the subject of what's yours and what's mine."

—Stieg Larsson

Do you feel burned out trying to keep other people happy? Do you let others walk all over you because you're afraid to stand up for yourself?

Often we don't say NO to people, because we're afraid it might offend them or create tension in a relationship.

We're taught to be kind to others, but we ultimately need to find the balance between being kind and being firm. Otherwise, we give others permission to take advantage of us.

You might hear the word "boundaries" and imagine walls that separate you from other people. In a sense, that's true.

But boundaries aren't necessarily a bad thing. In fact, they're an important ingredient in healthy, balanced relationships.

They're also a crucial part of maintaining your identity, mental health, and physical well-being.

When I set boundaries and stick to them, I find that I have more time and energy to put towards the things and people I love.

Standing up for yourself and your time can make a huge impact on your well-being and life satisfaction.

Healthy boundaries are the limits you place around your time, emotions, body, and mental health to stay resilient, solid, and content with who you are. These empowering borders protect you from being used, drained, or manipulated by others.

You can set boundaries around-

Emotional health

Time

Personal space

Morals and ethics

Material possessions and finances

Social media

Boundaries can be set with-

Family

Friends

Romantic relationships

Coworkers

Strangers

Putting yourself first can be a challenge, but now is the time to do so. Learning to set boundaries can be a valuable skill that helps you heal and enriches your relationships in the future.

Putting yourself first can be a challenge, but now is the time to do so. Learning to set boundaries can be a valuable skill that helps you heal and enriches your relationships in the future.

Polite NO is a full sentence. It is not an action to be undertaken only at certain times; it is a lifelong habit that we need to diligently practice in order to achieve our goals in work and life.

Appreciate Yourself More

"Self-appreciation is the foundation of life. Instead of looking for external approval, appreciate yourself more."

—Gustavo Razzetti

Sometimes it's more difficult to see what's right about ourselves than what's wrong. For some of us even thinking about our positive traits makes us uncomfortable. Praise and compliments can make us squirm, and we often don't know how to respond without self-consciousness.

Our life is like a house. There's nothing wrong with dreaming about having nicer windows or changing the colours of the walls. But if the foundation is not strong enough, the house won't hold the *weight*, it will collapse.

When you dream to become someone else, you stop valuing who you are.

Self-appreciation is the foundation of a happy life. Without it, you can't build a bigger you.

Sometimes we take self appreciation as selfish or me centred behaviour. But, based on my own experiences, I can assure you that self-appreciation is not the same as self-pity or self-indulgence, it doesn't mean living in a *me centred world.*

Self-growth is about becoming the best version of yourself, not someone else.

Appreciating who you are is the secret for a strong foundation, you can build on top of what you already are.

Self-Appreciation is not self-esteem, as I explain here, it's not about feeling special but accepting your uniqueness instead.

It's not about becoming someone different but appreciating who you already are. You are at peace with your own company, you acknowledge your beliefs, trust your instincts, and accept both your flaws and successes.

We usually focus more on negative thoughts rather than positive ones, that's why we narrow our inner-perception. We either get stuck on that negative self-image or exaggerate our good traits to offset negativity.

Practicing positive self-talk and being more appreciative can expand your inner-perception. You create new neural pathways that lead to positive thoughts.

Being compassionate and loving ourselves, is not only the foundation of our lives, it's the foundation of a better world. The stronger it is, the more we can build together.

The world needs *you.* Don't succumb to the external pressure to be someone else, become the best version of yourself. Appreciate yourself more.

VALUE YOURSELF BY VALUING YOUR TIME

"When you understand the value of time, the resource and the wealth of time, you will be running away from the crowd."

—Sunday Adelaja

Time is infinite, but your personal time on this earth is not. These words often ring through my head when I find myself procrastinating on a project or goal.

With so many distractions thrown at us on a daily basis, it's easy to lose sight of the big picture. Sometimes this is unavoidable.

But if we constantly get distracted by things like social media and other people's priorities, we become frustrated and stressed because we're not attending to our own wants and needs.

We all have a limited amount of time on this planet to do what we want to do and fulfil the dreams we want to turn into reality because once it's gone, it's gone.

However, by learning how to value our time, we can be proactive in making sure we're spending it and our energy in the right places, which means we're able to focus on what's important and what's meaningful to us.

One of the biggest mistakes we make in life is having a poor use of our time.

It is true that many of us have jobs and commitments, but how we choose to spend that time as well as our own free time plays a large role in our sense of fulfillment.

Some people create goals in the hopes of gaining more pleasure, others choose to find something they enjoy and spend as much time as they can on it, and some choose to linger around trying to fill the void of time with whatever entertains them at the moment.

Just as lingering around and wasting time does nothing to make us happier, Where our pleasure begins to fade away occurs when we lose touch with our sense of fulfillment, growth and adventure.

One of the first things we need to understand is whether we are filling our free time with activities to merely eliminate boredom or if we are spending that time on the activities, which make us better, give us new experiences, expand our knowledge and improve our lives in new emotionally fulfilling and purposeful ways.

Living purposefully doesn't mean doing something just because someone else tells you it's important and purposeful, it means doing what brings you a sense of pleasure and fulfillment.

I've seen both ends of the spectrum and can say spending your time on activities that bring you pleasure and fulfillment are some of the best experiences you can give yourself.

At one time in my life I spent nearly a year traveling the new places, exploring new cultures, trying new things and reading anything that would help me improve my life, and I felt that I was living my purpose and experiencing life to the fullest.

Focus on the few things that really matter to you and slowly eliminate the rest.

A careful balance of life long activities and short-term growth creating and fulfilling activities is the best way to go.

And remember, more time doesn't always equal a happier or more pleasurable life if you don't fill it with something you enjoy.

DISCOVER YOUR CORE VALUES

"A highly developed values system is like a compass. It serves as a guide to point you in the right direction when you are lost."

—Idowu Koyenikan

As a life coach, I appreciate the power of values.

I have worked with people of all ages, and that has given me the unique experience of learning about the different value systems of many people. It has been very interesting to listen to every person's story and what is important in their life, whether they are 5 or 65 years old.

Based on my own personal experiences and coaching sessions, I've noticed that individuals experience greater fulfillment when they live by their values.

And when we don't honor our values, our mental, emotional, and physical state suffers. I've seen this to be true in my life too.

In a world that is constantly evolving and taking new forms, it can be somewhat overwhelming trying to make sense of this thing called life.

One of the things that rarely changes in this world and what can provide a guiding light for you throughout your life are your core values.

Values reflect our sense of right and wrong. They help us grow and develop. They help us create the future we want. The decisions we make every day are a reflection of our values.

We learn most of our values from our parents and extended families. Our family values stem from our social and cultural values. Sometimes new life experiences may change values we previously held.

In today's world, it may seem our society doesn't practice many values. We have a rise in discrimination, abuse of power, greed, etc. What are we leaving behind for our future generations?

Maybe it's time society takes a hard look at its values like Empathy, respect, love, loyalty, honesty, compassion, care, attention and many more.

Values can be contagious; if you practice them, many others will also, including our children. Hopefully more practice from all of us will leave the world a better place for future generations.

Patience attracts happiness

"Patience and perseverance have a magical effect before which difficulties disappear and obstacles vanish."- John Quincy Adams

What are the main qualities you need to inculcate to be successful at work?

Hard work is one of them.

Reliability is another.

But one quality that is just as important but not discussed as often is patience.

With the digital era at its peak, everything has become faster, simpler, and more convenient.

Nowadays, when we're feeling hungry, we don't have to go through the painstaking process of preparing ingredients or mixing them in a pan, and washing the dishes afterward.

A few taps on our phones is all it takes to get food delivered to us within the hour.

If we're missing someone and want to see them right away, we no longer have to wait for one or both of our schedules to clear up or travel great distances to see them. We have numerous video calling face time apps.

With advanced technology, we enjoy instant gratification and have come to expect it like a basic right.

At the same time, unfortunately, we are slowly forgetting what it means to be patient.

The road to success is a long one. It's not something that can be achieved overnight. It's rather a slow but promising process of growth that, with enough perseverance, meets the threshold of success.

As we all know that Michael Jordan has missed more than 9000 shots and lost almost 300 games? If he lacked patience, he wouldn't have become one of the greatest basketball players of all time.

Failure fuels our pursuit, and patience keeps us from quitting. By being patient, we learn from our mistakes, become better at what we do, and eventually achieve the greatness we've been striving for all along.

Some of us are innately patient. Some of us are not. It's important to recognize this and stop ourselves when we are exuding impatience.

We should make a conscious effort to be more patient. Remember, all good things take time!

Create Perfect Solitude

"Solitude is a catalyst for innovation."

—Mahatma Gandhi

Recently, I spent a morning reviewing my goals and the things I'd like to accomplish over the next several months.

As I sat on a quiet park bench looking out at a magnificent sun rise on a beautiful winter morning, I was reminded of how valuable and how meaningful, it is to take time to retreat and withdraw, both for my task list *and for my spirit.*

The practice of solitude brings **clarity of thought**, a **time for reflection**, and a **break from the noise** and although we know we *should take time* to focus on this important discipline.

First, realize that finding solitude will be difficult. Every part of our society is structured to discourage quiet alone time.

Advertisers, apps, TV, friends and friends, they all want our attention. This environment has made all of us deeply uncomfortable with being alone in silence.

Our neural pathways have been strengthened by years of external stimulation to crave more of it.

Our lives and our future depends on breaking this cycle. Discovering our highest purpose and the best way for us to serve the world, comes only through turning inward, not in forcing one more item onto your to-do list.

Physical exercise is solitude's best buddy. When you strap on your shoes or climb onto your bike and leave the house to explore the world, your mind quiets and you get a new perspective on your life and all of its complications. You can't get this sitting at a desk.

To ensure your exercise generates the solitude we're seeking:

- Go alone.
- Don't listen to music or audiobooks.
- Leave your phone at home.
- Get into nature if possible, away from others.
- Skip the treadmill and other equipments.

Make it a time to look forward to. Treat yourself to your favourite cappuccino or that Chai Tea you love.

Dress in your favorite clothes, or stop by your favorite breakfast place on the way.

Do what you need to do to make the experience special and rewarding.

It's been my experience that there is a "recipe" for creating great moments and it begins with the simplest of things.

It probably goes without saying, but during this time of solitude, you should be intentional.

Turn off your phone. Resist the temptation to check your email right before you get started. If you have a thought that leads you to look something up online, make a note and do it later.

In our digital world, true solitude comes from completely disconnecting from everything around you, not just being physically alone.

Don't head off to the nature for a morning and then never do it again.

The key to the practice of solitude is to engage in a rhythm of engagement and withdraw. Once you get in a rhythm, you'll probably want to do it once a month, but start with whatever you feel is comfortable.

Cultivate Self Discipline

""I think self-discipline is something, it's like a muscle. The more you exercise it, the stronger it gets."

—Daniel Goldstein

One of the most important life skills to develop, for those just starting out in life is the skill of self-discipline.

It's like a superpower.

When I developed some self-discipline, I started exercising and eating healthier and meditating and writing more, I started a blog and wrote articles, I read more and work earlier, I decluttered and transformed my finances. I'm far from perfect, but I've learned a lot.

But if you don't develop self-discipline, it causes problems, health problems, distraction, procrastination, financial problems, clutter, things piling up and overwhelming you, and much more.

So it's such an important skill to develop, but most people don't know where to start.

I'm writing it for myself, and for anyone else who would like to develop a superpower.

Studies show that those with higher levels of self-control have higher self-esteem, less binge eating and alcohol abuse, better relationships and interpersonal skills, and more optimal emotional responses.

Others show that those with self-discipline are more content, satisfied and happy.

Everyone has the power to grow their self-discipline. Showing up right here, right now is already supporting that goal, as well as the bigger one of becoming happier and healthier.

These easy steps can help us get out of a self-control mindset and lean more into mindfulness. Remember, all it takes is time, compassion, and focus.

Build routines- The easiest way to practice self-discipline is to avoid making on-the-fly decisions. We can do this by building routines.

Write it down- We can keep notes on our phones, write on sticky notes or keep a small notebook at our desks. Simply writing the situation, our immediate thought and the resulting emotions can help us distance ourselves from what's top of mind.

Get more sleep- If we're getting less than 6 hours a night, our brains won't be able to recruit the systems needed for impulse control. To best support our goals, our brains need a good sleep of at least 7 hours.

Practice self-compassion- Flexibility is just as necessary as discipline when creating a healthy routine. Instead of being hard on ourselves, we can treat ourselves compassionately and allow ourselves to adjust our plans.

Admittedly, it is hard to commit to self-discipline everyday. Self-discipline is no easy feat because we are constantly faced with issues that seem to occur at the most bothersome time.

It is true that we have no control over what can happen but we do have control over how we react to what happens. We also have access and opportunity to practice techniques that enable us to exercise self-discipline and reach our vision.

Spread Kindness & Develop Empathy

"Love and kindness are never wasted. They always make a difference. They bless the one who receives them, and they bless you, the giver."

—Barbara De Angelis

In the morning, I was thinking about the importance of core values and how we use them in our daily life and while writing about kindness and empathy, I remembered a beautiful story of a grandmother and her grandson relation filled with love, care and kindness. I'm sharing it with you all.

An elderly woman and her little grandson, whose face was sprinkled with bright freckles, spent the day at the zoo. Lots of children were waiting in line to get their cheeks painted by a local artist who was decorating them with tiger paws.

"You've got so many freckles, there's no place to paint!" a girl in the line said to the little fella.

Embarrassed, the little boy dropped his head. His grandmother knelt down next to him. "I love your freckles. When I was a little girl I always wanted freckles," she said, while tracing her finger across the child's cheek.

"Freckles are beautiful." The boy looked up, "Really?"

"Of course," said the grandmother. "Why just name me one thing that's prettier than freckles."

The little boy thought for a moment, peered intensely into his grandma's face and softly whispered, "Wrinkles.

More and more, we live in bubbles. Most of us are surrounded by people who look like us, earn like us, spend money like us, have educations like us and worship like us. The result is an empathy deficit, and it's at the root of many of our biggest problems.

So what is empathy?

It's understanding how others feel and being compassionate toward them. It happens when two parts of the brain work together, the emotional center perceives the feelings of others and the cognitive center tries to understand why they feel that way and how we can be helpful to them.

Some people are more naturally empathetic than others, but there are easy, yet with simple exercises that anyone can do to increase their empathy.

Don't just stand in someone else's shoes, as the saying goes, but take a walk in them. Spend time in a new neighborhood, or strike up a conversation with a homeless person in your community.

Positive psychology is dedicated to researching what makes individuals and communities flourish. Popular positive psychology techniques include random acts of kindness, like:

- **Paying it forward** – treat someone to something, like buying a cup of coffee for the person behind you in the café queue
- **Sending notes of gratitude** – hand-write a thank you note to someone you admire or who has helped you out
- **Post a sticky note** – stick post-it notes with nice messages written on them around your house or somewhere in public
- **Volunteering** – being a volunteer helps others and is good for you too
- **Donating to a charity store** – help people out by giving away what you no longer want or need
- **Smiling at strangers** – smiling is contagious and it makes you feel good if people smile back
- **Letting people know you love what they do** – this could be someone you know or people you admire, like a writer or musician.

Let us focus on the people around us. Give them a helping hand and find perfect joy in it.

GIVE BACK, FOR NO REASON AT ALL

"If you're not reaching back to help anyone then you're not building a legacy."

—Germany Kent

There is a Chinese saying that goes: "If you want happiness for an hour, take a nap. If you want happiness for a day, go fishing. If you want happiness for a year, inherit a fortune. If you want happiness for a lifetime, help somebody."

For centuries, the greatest thinkers have suggested the same thing: Happiness is found in helping others.

Life's most persistent and urgent question is: what are you doing for others?— Martin Luther King, Jr.

When I first read this quote, I immediately thought, *What* am *I doing for others? What am I doing on a daily basis to make the world a more positive place?*

What I love most about what I do for work is that I have the power to positively impact the lives of others online. I have the opportunity to reach out to others and share what I've learned about living a more positive, more present life.

I would love to share a lovely story of immense kindness with you all, I read in moralstories26, that inspired me a lot to give something back to society…Must read

One day an elderly postman knocked on the door of a house and said, "Take your letter."

A little girl's voice echoed from inside, "I am coming.. Please wait."

But even after 5 minutes no one came. Postman asked again.

Girl replied, "Uncle, if you are in a hurry, put the letter under the door.

The postman replied, "No, I'm waiting. It's a registered mail, so someone's signature is also needed."

After 10 minutes the door opened. Postman was angry about the delay. He was about to shout, but as soon as the door opened, he was shocked to see that in front of him, was a little handicapped girl who had no legs.

Postman quietly gave the letter and left.

Little girl lives alone in her house. Her mother expired and father used to work far away. To take care of the girl, a maid used to stay with her in the morning and evening, but she used to stay alone in the house.

In a month or two whenever mail came the postman patiently waited and shared with her. Gradually interaction and compassion grew.

Little girl noticed that the postman used to come with badly torn shoes.

Rainy season came. One day when the postman left after giving a letter to girl, his shoe prints were left on wet soil. Girl took the picture of shoe print. Next day, she asked the maid to get shoes of that size.

Diwali was about to come. He bought a small chocolate for little girl. Next day he went to little girl's house and handed her chocolate and said, "Take this small gift from uncle's side."

Girl was happy to get that and asked the postman to wait. After a while, she bought a box and handed it to the postman, she said, "Uncle, this is a gift from my side to you."

Postman was surprised to see the box. He asked, "You're like daughter to me, how can I accept a gift from you?"

Little girl insisted and said, " Uncle please accept the gift. I'll be happy."

"Ok", said the old man and kept his hand on her head with lots of blessings.

When the postman opened the box, he was surprised to see the pair of shoes in it. Next day the postman reached the post office and pleaded to the postmaster that he should be transferred to another area.

When the postmaster asked for a reason. He told him everything with wet eyes and said, "Sir, from today I will not be able to go to the street. The little girl saw my torn shoes and gave me shoes, but how will I able to give her foot.?" and burst into tears.

We all have the power to do something kind for others, to make the world a better place by taking positive action.

There is greatness and beauty in making time, especially when it's inconvenient, for the sake of someone nearby.

You don't have to tell people that you care, just show them. In your relationships and interactions with others, nothing you can give is more appreciated than your sincere, focused attention.

Being with someone, listening without a clock and without anticipation of results is the ultimate compliment. It is indeed the most valued gesture you can make to another human being.

So give someone the gift of YOU, your time, undivided attention and kindness. That's better than any other gift, it won't break or get lost, and will always be remembered.

You have the ability to show people how amazing they are, just the way they are. So act on this ability without hesitation and don't forget to show yourself the same courtesy.

Doing things for others, whether small, unplanned acts or regular volunteering is a powerful way to boost our happiness and those around us. The people we help may be strangers, family, friends, colleagues, or neighbors.

Giving isn't just about money. Giving can be as simple as a single kind word, a smile, or a thoughtful gesture. It can include giving time, love, care, skills, or attention. Sometimes these mean as much, if not more, than financial gifts.

Compassion and kindness towards others is the glue that connects individual happiness with the community and societal wellbeing. Giving to others helps us connect with people and meets one of our basic human needs-relatedness.

Kindness is the key to creating a happier, more trusting and beautiful community.

SUMMARY

Life is beautiful, it's always been. People just think it doesn't because of the different perspectives they have and the negative emotions they experience in life. However, bear in mind that hardship is just part of living life, it is not the whole part.

For me, connection with my life means feeling in alignment with my highest self, it's feeling capable, strong, loving and compassionate. It's a sense of knowingness and wisdom that is completely unique to me.

It's so easy to go through the ins and outs of life and forget some of the important things. Connection for me is important. I'm not going to judge myself for feeling disconnected, but instead, focus on things that I can do to get back in touch with myself.

You live with yourself every day. So why would you need to pause and connect with yourself?

The truth is that human brains are mysterious. We can trick ourselves, hide from ourselves, and do things without knowing the motivation why. The more disconnected we get from ourselves, the harder it is to know why we do the things that we do.

The result can be feelings of pointlessness, hopelessness, and vague unhappiness.

In contrast, if you make the effort to connect with yourself, you reap the benefits. You feel like you are able to live in line with your own values. You know what you want, why you want it, and how to achieve it.

In this chaotic world it's easy to get lost in the mix and often we have to reconnect and rediscover ourselves. In the end, your life has always been about YOU and your journey.

It's not only about the things we do but how we live our lives. Reconnecting with yourself and how you find your Joy and Bliss is different for everyone. Only you know what steps help you the most.

When you dedicate yourself to living life to the fullest, you feel like you can overcome anything. Each day is an opportunity for greatness, and you feel fresh and ready to find it. It's amazing what a little positivity can do to a person's entire outlook.

Engage in pursuits that bring you joy. Because it is your life and no one else's, you should live it the way you want.

Life is full of opportunity. Remember, always aim for a fulfilling life, not a richer life full of fear of losing something less valuable than life. Forget your past and worry about the future, just live in the present and appreciate the beauty of living.

You only have one opportunity to do this successfully, so make the most of it. If you take advantage of everything that life has to offer, you'll not only have a better time, but you'll also be an example to those around you.

Therefore, make it a point to reconnect with your life fully, because it is the most valuable gift you possess.